Published by Around J Srls
Via Avogadro 12/A
10121 Torino
info@around-j.com
http://www.around-j.com/

Printed by Amazon
"Only the brave #OTB"
ISBN 978-88-943100-0-9

Dear Alessia & Giulia

Every year, at the end of the summer, I take some time just for me and write down what I want to achieve in the next year. I contemplate my personal goals, and more importantly, what I want to become. And while my goals may change year after year, this always makes the top of my list: Be your personal hero.

This goal becomes more and more challenging to achieve as you grow up and your expectations of me rise, but it gives me the right motivation to improve day after day to always be better in front of your eyes.

The best part of my day is in the morning – when I snuggle into your bed while you're still sleeping, maybe still dreaming, and wake you up with cuddles. My favourite days are Saturday and Sunday, when we get to stay in bed to talk and play before breakfast. And we talk about everything – life, goals, dreams, love, happiness, and much more.

As this book comes into the world, you're 8 and 10 years old – feisty and sprightly, with vivid imaginations, pursuing what you want with wild abandon, and your entire lives ahead of you. The reason I made this book for you is so that you'll always have a physical reminder that life may not always be easy, but you're the captain and you can (and must) steer the course to anywhere you dream of going. The sayings and quotes in this book are the ones that have served as my guide as I navigate my own life, and work hard to be the best man and father I can be for you both.

While all these sayings and quotes are perfect for our morning talks in your bed, I also aspire for them to not just inspire you towards the milestones of your lives, but inspire everyone who reads them and is seeking that little extra push towards achieving great things.

Finally, my dear Alessia and Giulia, I want you to know that you're never too young – or too old – to realise your dreams. And always remember that your mindset, not your age, determines your success. And success comes to Only The Brave.

RULE #1: NEVER BE #2.

#OTB

IT'S BETTER TO DIE OF PASSION THAN OF BOREDOM.

· ·

LIVE FOR THE MOMENTS YOU CAN'T PUT INTO WORDS.

#OTB

YOU DIDN'T WAKE UP TO BE AVERAGE.

. . . .

DON'T HAVE DREAMS, HAVE GOALS.

. . . .

WHAT WOULD YOU DO IF YOU WEREN'T AFRAID?
#OTB

YOUR MIND MUST ARRIVE AT
YOUR DESTINATION BEFORE
YOUR LIFE DOES.

A LOT OF PEOPLE ARE AFRAID
TO SAY WHAT THEY WANT.
THAT'S WHY THEY DON'T GET
WHAT THEY WANT.
#OTB

A GOAL WITHOUT A PLAN IS JUST A WISH.

DON'T WAIT FOR OPPORTUNITIES, CREATE THEM.

DREAM BIG, WORK HARD. BE KIND. STAY HUMBLE.
#OTB

WHATEVER YOU ARE, BE A GOOD ONE.

#OTB

YOUR FOCUS DETERMINES YOUR REALITY.

. . . .

YOU GET WHAT YOU WORK FOR, NOT WHAT YOU WISH FOR. IT ONLY TAKES ONE PERSON TO CHANGE YOUR LIFE. YOU.

#OTB

GIVE YOURSELF PERMISSION TO LIVE A BIG LIFE.

. . . .

STEP INTO WHO YOU ARE MEANT TO BE.
STOP PLAYING SMALL; YOU ARE MEANT FOR GREATER THINGS.
#OTB

ALWAYS REMEMBER
YOU ARE
BRAVER THAN YOU BELIEVE,
STRONGER THAN YOU SEEM,
AND SMARTER
THAN YOU THINK.
#OTB

GOALS DETERMINE WHAT YOU'RE GOING TO BE.

· ·

YOU ARE NOT A PRODUCT OF YOUR CIRCUMSTANCES. YOU ARE A PRODUCT OF YOUR DECISIONS.

#OTB

IF WHAT YOU WANT DOESN'T EXIST, CREATE IT.

#OTB

UNTIL YOU BUY INTO YOUR OWN DREAMS, PEOPLE WILL KEEP SELLING YOU THEIRS.

························

WE ARE WHAT WE REPEATEDLY DO. EXCELLENCE, THEN, IS NOT AN ACT, BUT A HABIT.
#OTB

TRAVEL OFTEN. GETTING LOST WILL HELP YOU FIND YOURSELF.

. . . .

ALL ROADS THAT LED TO SUCCESS HAVE TO PASS THROUGH HARD WORK BOULEVARD.
#OTB

AFTER CLIMBING A GREAT HILL, ONE ONLY FINDS THAT THERE ARE MANY MORE HILLS TO CLIMB.
#OTB

YOU MAY STRUGGLE, BUT YOU SHOULD NEVER QUIT.

YOU MAY HAVE TO FIGHT A BATTLE MORE THAN ONCE TO WIN IT.
#OTB

DON'T LET ANYTHING STOP YOU FROM REACHING YOUR GOAL.

. . . .

SUCCESS IS INEVITABLE IF YOU NEVER GIVE UP.
#OTB

ONCE YOU FIND SOMETHING YOU LOVE TO DO, BE THE BEST AT DOING IT.

....

PEOPLE WHO ARE CRAZY ENOUGH TO THINK THEY CAN CHANGE THE WORLD, ARE THE ONES WHO DO.

#OTB

PEOPLE WHO SUCCEED HAVE
MOMENTUM. THE MORE THEY
SUCCEED,
THE MORE THEY
WANT TO SUCCEED,
AND THE MORE THEY
FIND A WAY TO SUCCEED.

SIMILARLY, WHEN SOMEONE IS
FAILING, THE TENDENCY IS TO GET
ON A DOWNWARD SPIRAL
THAT CAN EVEN BECOME A SELF-
FULFILLING PROPHECY.
#OTB

AN AVERAGE PERSON WITH AVERAGE TALENTS AND AMBITION AND AVERAGE EDUCATION, CAN OUTSTRIP THE MOST BRILLIANT GENIUS IN OUR SOCIETY, IF THAT PERSON HAS CLEAR, FOCUSED GOALS.

#OTB

AMBITION IS THE FIRST STEP TOWARD SUCCESS.

· ·

RAISE THE BAR A LITTLE MORE EVERY DAY.

· ·

DON'T QUIT. YOU DIDN'T COME THIS FAR TO ONLY COME THIS FAR.
#OTB

YOU DON'T DECIDE YOUR
FUTURE. YOU
DECIDE YOUR HABITS AND
YOUR HABITS
DECIDE YOUR FUTURE.

YOU DON'T FIND WHO YOU
ARE, CREATE
WHO YOU ARE.
#OTB

YOU GET WHAT YOU FOCUS ON, SO FOCUS ON WHAT YOU WANT.

· ·

YOU CAN HAVE ANYTHING YOU WANT IN THIS LIFE IF YOU'RE WILLING TO WORK FOR IT.
#OTB

THE STARTING POINT OF ALL ACHIEVEMENT IS DESIRE.

....

IT ALWAYS SEEMS IMPOSSIBLE UNTIL IT'S DONE.

#OTB

ALL OUR DREAMS CAN COME TRUE IF WE HAVE THE COURAGE TO PURSUE THEM.

. . . .

A JOURNEY OF A THOUSAND MILES MUST BEGIN WITH A SINGLE STEP.

#OTB

FIND A WAY
OR MAKE ONE.

· ·

EVERY DAY, YOU'RE EITHER
BUILDING YOUR DREAMS OR
SOMEONE ELSE'S.

· ·

GOALS ARE DREAMS WITH
DEADLINES.
#OTB

SET A GOAL THAT MAKES YOU WANT TO JUMP OUT OF BED IN THE MORNING.

. . . .

PEOPLE RARELY SUCCEED UNLESS THEY HAVE FUN IN WHAT THEY ARE DOING.

#OTB

THERE IS NO ELEVATOR TO SUCCESS. YOU HAVE TO TAKE THE STAIRS.

#OTB

LIMITATIONS LIVE ONLY IN YOUR MIND. BUT IF YOU USE YOUR IMAGINATION, YOUR POSSIBILITIES BECOME LIMITLESS.

#OTB

YOUR ATTITUDE DETERMINES YOUR ALTITUDE.

. . . .

A RIVER CUTS THROUGH ROCK, NOT BECAUSE OF ITS POWER, BUT ITS PERSISTENCE.

#OTB

ALL PROGRESS TAKES PLACE OUTSIDE THE COMFORT ZONE.

#OTB

YOU WILL NOT SUCCEED
BECAUSE YOU ARE
EXCEPTIONALLY
TALENTED BUT BECAUSE
YOU ARE EXCEPTIONALLY
DETERMINED TO
ACHIEVE YOUR GOALS.

. . . .

IF IT DOESN'T
MAKE YOU HAPPY,
MAKE YOU MONEY OR
MAKE YOU BETTER,
DON'T MAKE TIME FOR IT.

#OTB

DON'T FORGET TO SMILE.

....

NOTHING IS WORTH IT IF YOU AREN'T HAPPY.

#OTB

DON'T WAIT FOR THE PERFECT MOMENT. TAKE THE MOMENT AND MAKE IT PERFECT.

. . . .

A GOOD PLAN VIOLENTLY EXECUTED NOW IS BETTER THAN A PERFECT PLAN EXECUTED NEXT WEEK.

#OTB

LOST TIME IS NEVER FOUND AGAIN.
ALL GREAT ACHIEVEMENTS REQUIRE TIME.

#OTB

NEVER GIVE UP
ON A DREAM BECAUSE
OF THE TIME
IT WILL TAKE
TO ACCOMPLISH.

DON'T WAIT.
THE TIME WILL
NEVER BE JUST RIGHT.

#OTB

IF YOU NEVER TRY, YOU'LL NEVER KNOW.

. . . .

IF YOU WAIT UNTIL YOU'RE READY, YOU'LL BE WAITING FOR THE REST OF YOUR LIFE.

#OTB

IF YOU ARE NOT DOING WHAT YOU LOVE, YOU ARE WASTING YOUR TIME.

. . . .

ONE DAY, YOU WILL WAKE UP AND THERE WON'T BE ANY MORE TIME TO DO THE THING YOU'VE ALWAYS WANTED. DO IT NOW.

#OTB

NEVER GIVE UP ON SOMETHING JUST BECAUSE IT'S MORE DIFFICULT THAN YOU THOUGHT IT WOULD BE. GREAT THINGS TAKE TIME.

. . . .

EVERY OVERNIGHT SUCCESS IS TEN YEARS IN THE MAKING.
#OTB

TIME IS THE COIN OF
YOUR LIFE. IT IS THE ONLY COIN
YOU HAVE, AND ONLY
YOU CAN DETERMINE
HOW IT WILL BE SPENT.
BE CAREFUL LEST YOU
LET OTHER PEOPLE SPEND
IT FOR YOU.

. . . .

ONE DAY, ALL THOSE
LATE NIGHTS AND EARLY
MORNINGS WILL PAY OFF.
#OTB

YOU ARE WHAT YOU DO, NOT WHAT YOU SAY YOU'LL DO.

. . . .

THERE ARE NO TRAFFIC JAMS ALONG THE EXTRA MILE.
#OTB

GOOD THINGS COME TO PEOPLE WHO WAIT, BUT BETTER THINGS COME TO THOSE WHO GO OUT AND GET THEM.

· ·

VISION WITHOUT ACTION IS A DAYDREAM. ACTION WITHOUT VISION IS A NIGHTMARE.
#OTB

STOP WORRYING HOW IT'S GOING TO HAPPEN AND START BELIEVING THAT IT WILL.

OVER PROMISE, THEN OVER DELIVER.
#OTB

PUSH YOURSELF BECAUSE NO ONE IS GOING TO DO IT FOR YOU.

·······················

VISUALISE WHAT YOU WANT AND GO GET IT.
#OTB

BECOME THE HARDEST WORKING PERSON YOU KNOW.

· ·

LIFE SHRINKS OR EXPANDS IN PROPORTION TO ONE'S COURAGE.
#OTB

STOP WISHING.
START DOING.

....

LIVE EACH DAY
AS IF IT BE YOUR LAST.
#OTB

IF YOU WANT BIG THINGS, DON'T GET DISTRACTED BY THE SMALL THINGS.

DON'T LET SMALL MINDS CONVINCE YOU THAT YOUR DREAMS ARE TOO BIG.

STOP GETTING DISTRACTED BY THINGS THAT HAVE NOTHING TO DO WITH YOUR GOALS.

#OTB

SET GOALS SO BIG YOU GET UNCOMFORTABLE TELLING SMALL-MINDED PEOPLE ABOUT THEM.

....

THE MIND IS EVERYTHING. WHAT YOU THINK, YOU BECOME.
#OTB

YOU CAN'T GET TO THE NEXT LEVEL UNTIL YOU'RE COMFORTABLE BEING UNCOMFORTABLE.

#OTB

DON'T SET YOUR GOALS
BASED ON WHAT OTHERS
SAY YOU CAN DO.
SET THEM BASED
ON WHAT YOU
IMAGINE YOU CAN DO.

STOP LETTING YOUR
PAST CONTROL
YOUR FUTURE.
#OTB

GO CONFIDENTLY IN THE DIRECTION OF YOUR DREAMS AND LIVE THE LIFE YOU HAVE ALWAYS IMAGINED.

#OTB

YOUR CONFIDENCE DETERMINES:
THE SIZE OF GOALS YOU UNDERTAKE;
HOW LIKELY YOU WILL ACHIEVE THOSE GOALS;
HOW WELL YOU WILL BOUNCE BACK FROM FAILURES.
#OTB

SUCCESS TAKES TWO THINGS: CONSISTENCY AND DEDICATION.

. . . .

IF YOU ARE PERSISTENT, YOU WILL GET IT.
IF YOU ARE CONSISTENT, YOU WILL KEEP IT.
#OTB

WHEN YOU HAVE CONFIDENCE, YOU CAN HAVE A LOT OF FUN.
AND WHEN YOU HAVE FUN, YOU CAN DO AMAZING THINGS.

....

OPTIMISM IS THE FAITH THAT LEADS TO ACHIEVEMENT. NOTHING CAN BE DONE WITHOUT HOPE AND CONFIDENCE.

#OTB

WITH CONFIDENCE, YOU HAVE WON BEFORE YOU HAVE STARTED.

....

IF YOU WANT SOMETHING YOU'VE NEVER HAD, DO SOMETHING YOU'VE NEVER DONE.

#OTB

DON'T SETTLE FOR ORDINARY — BECOME EXTRAORDINARY.

· ·

WHEN NO ONE BELIEVES IN YOU, BELIEVE IN YOURSELF.
#OTB

CREATE A LIFE FROM WHICH YOU DON'T NEED A VACATION.

. . . .

AT FIRST THEY WILL LAUGH AT YOUR DREAMS. THEN THEY WILL ASK IF YOU'RE HIRING.

#OTB

FOLLOW YOUR DREAMS, OR YOU WILL SPEND THE REST OF YOUR LIFE WORKING FOR SOMEONE ELSE WHO DID.

....

PEOPLE THAT HAVE GIVEN UP ON THEIR DREAMS WILL NEVER UNDERSTAND YOURS.
#OTB

REFUSE TO LOWER YOUR STANDARD FOR THOSE WHO REFUSE TO RAISE THEIRS. YOU SET THE BAR.

. . . .

STAY AWAY FROM NEGATIVE PEOPLE. THEY HAVE A PROBLEM FOR EVERY SOLUTION.
#OTB

WINNERS FOCUS ON WINNING. LOSERS FOCUS ON WINNERS.

....

SIT WITH WINNERS — THE CONVERSATION WILL BE DIFFERENT.
#OTB

POSITIVE PEOPLE
ALSO HAVE
NEGATIVE THOUGHTS.
THEY JUST DON'T LET
THOSE THOUGHTS
GROW AND DESTROY THEM.

. . . .

IF YOU CAN'T BUILD
WITH THEM,
DON'T CHILL WITH THEM.
#OTB

THE LESS YOU
RESPOND TO NEGATIVE
PEOPLE, THE MORE PEACEFUL
YOUR LIFE WILL BECOME.

YOUR VIBES ATTRACT
YOUR TRIBE.

INVEST IN PEOPLE
WHO INVEST IN YOU.
#OTB

LIFE IS ABOUT THE PEOPLE YOU MEET, AND THE THINGS YOU CREATE WITH THEM.

. . . .

WHEN SOMEONE TELLS YOU SOMETHING CAN'T BE DONE, IT'S A REFLECTION OF THEIR LIMITATIONS NOT YOURS.
#OTB

WHEN WRITING THE STORY OF YOUR LIFE, DON'T LET ANYONE ELSE HOLD THE PEN.

. . . .

UNSUCCESSFUL PEOPLE HAVE GREAT IDEAS. SUCCESSFUL PEOPLE HAVE GREAT EXECUTION.
#OTB

LEARN THE RULES LIKE A PRO, SO THAT YOU CAN BREAK THEM AS AN ARTIST.

. . . .

IT'S NOT ABOUT IDEAS; IT'S ABOUT MAKING IDEAS HAPPEN.
#OTB

YOU'RE NOT FOR EVERYONE. JUST BE YOU AND THE RIGHT PEOPLE WILL COME INTO YOUR LIFE.

....

WINNING ISN'T EVERYTHING, BUT WANTING TO WIN IS.
#OTB

WHEN THE WRONG
PEOPLE LEAVE YOUR LIFE,
THE RIGHT THINGS
START HAPPENING.

. . . .

WINNERS FIND A
WAY, LOSERS
FIND EXCUSE.
#OTB

GREAT PEOPLE TALK ABOUT
IDEAS. AVERAGE PEOPLE
TALK ABOUT THINGS.
SMALL PEOPLE TALK ABOUT
OTHER PEOPLE.

· ·

SUCCESSFUL PEOPLE
SET LONG-TERM GOALS,
AND THEY KNOW THESE AIMS ARE
MERELY THE RESULT
OF SHORT-TERM HABITS THAT THEY
NEED TO DO EVERY DAY.
#OTB

SURROUND YOURSELF WITH PEOPLE WHOM YOU WANT TO BE LIKE.

HANG OUT WITH PEOPLE WHO FORCE YOU TO LEVEL UP.
#OTB

EVERYONE'S SELF-MADE. ONLY THE SUCCESSFUL WILL ADMIT IT.

· ·

IF YOU'RE THE SMARTEST PERSON IN THE ROOM, YOU ARE IN THE WRONG ROOM.
#OTB

A GREAT PERSON ATTRACTS GREAT PEOPLE AND KNOWS HOW TO HOLD THEM TOGETHER.

. . . .

THE GREATEST PLEASURE IN LIFE IS DOING WHAT PEOPLE SAY YOU CANNOT DO.

#OTB

DON'T STOP WHEN YOU'RE TIRED, STOP WHEN YOU'RE DONE.

. . . .

EVERYONE WANTS TO BE SUCCESSFUL UNTIL THEY SEE HOW MUCH WORK IS REQUIRED.
#OTB

A LOT OF PEOPLE HAVE IDEAS,
BUT THERE ARE FEW WHO
DECIDE TO DO SOMETHING
ABOUT THEM NOW. NOT TOMORROW.
NOT NEXT WEEK.
BUT TODAY.

A GOOD LEADER IS
A PERSON WHO TAKES A LITTLE
MORE THAN HIS
SHARE OF THE BLAME AND A LITTLE
LESS THAN HIS SHARE OF THE
CREDIT.
#OTB

IMPOSSIBLE IS A WORD TO BE FOUND ONLY IN THE DICTIONARY OF FOOLS.

. . . .

THE ONLY PLACE WHERE SUCCESS COMES BEFORE WORK IS IN THE DICTIONARY.

#OTB

DON'T RAISE YOUR VOICE; IMPROVE YOUR ARGUMENT.

DON'T WISH IT WAS EASIER; GET BETTER.
#OTB

IN ORDER TO BE IRREPLACEABLE, ONE MUST ALWAYS BE DIFFERENT.

· ·

IF YOU WANT TO FLY, YOU HAVE TO GIVE UP THE THINGS THAT WEIGH YOU DOWN.
#OTB

WINNERS ARE NOT PEOPLE WHO NEVER FAIL, BUT PEOPLE WHO NEVER QUIT.

FOR EVERY EXCUSE SOMEONE MAKES, THERE IS ANOTHER PERSON OVERCOMING THAT EXCUSE AND BECOMING SUCCESSFUL.
#OTB

HAVE YOU EVER MET A HATER DOING BETTER THAN YOU?

#OTB

YOUR ENERGY INTRODUCES YOU BEFORE YOU EVEN SPEAK.

....

BE THE ENERGY YOU WANT TO ATTRACT.
#OTB

DON'T BE PUSHED BY YOUR PROBLEMS, BE LED BY YOUR DREAMS.

WHEN YOU FOCUS ON PROBLEMS, YOU WILL HAVE MORE PROBLEMS. WHEN YOU FOCUS ON POSSIBILITIES, YOU WILL HAVE MORE OPPORTUNITIES.
#OTB

LIFE IS TOO SHORT TO BE LIVING SOMEBODY ELSE'S DREAM.

. . . .

BEAUTIFUL THINGS HAPPEN WHEN YOU DISTANCE YOURSELF FROM NEGATIVITY.
#OTB

BEFORE YOU ARE A LEADER, SUCCESS IS ALL ABOUT GROWING YOURSELF. WHEN YOU BECOME A LEADER, SUCCESS IS ALL ABOUT GROWING OTHERS.

#OTB

BE A VOICE,
NOT AN ECHO.

· ·

BE GRATEFUL
FOR WHAT YOU
HAVE WHILE WORKING
FOR WHAT YOU WANT.
#OTB

SUCCESS DOESN'T HAVE ANYTHING TO WITH THE OUTCOME. IT'S ALL IN THE PROCESS.

. . . .

IF YOU DON'T KNOW WHERE YOU ARE GOING, YOU WILL PROBABLY END UP SOMEWHERE ELSE.

#OTB

THE BEST WAY TO PREDICT THE FUTURE IS TO CREATE IT.

· ·

THE DIFFERENCE BETWEEN GOOD AND GREAT IS ATTENTION TO DETAIL.
#OTB

THE FUTURE BELONGS TO THE COMPETENT. GET GOOD, GET BETTER, BE THE BEST!

· ·

IF YOU DON'T HAVE ANY PROBLEMS, YOU CAN BE SURE THAT YOU ARE TRAVELLING IN A WRONG PATH.
#OTB

A PERSON WHO NEVER MADE A MISTAKE HAS NEVER TRIED ANYTHING NEW.

. . . .

ARISE, AWAKE, STOP NOT UNTIL YOUR GOAL IS ACHIEVED.
#OTB

ARRIVING AT ONE GOAL IS THE STARTING POINT TO ANOTHER.

· ·

DON'T BE AFRAID TO FAIL; BE AFRAID NOT TO TRY.
#OTB

BUILD YOUR OWN DREAMS, OR SOMEONE ELSE WILL HIRE YOU TO BUILD THEIRS.

. . . .

BE WITH SOMEONE WHO SUPPORTS YOUR DREAMS AND GOALS.
#OTB

DON'T EVER LET SOMEBODY TELL YOU, YOU CAN'T DO SOMETHING.

....

BELIEVE YOU CAN AND YOU'RE HALFWAY THERE.
#OTB

**MOTIVATION IS WHAT
GETS YOU STARTED.
HABIT IS WHAT KEEPS YOU GOING.**

....

**DON'T BE AFRAID OF
FAILURES. LEARN FROM
IT AND KEEP GOING.
PERSISTENCE IS WHAT
CREATES EXCELLENCE.**
#OTB

FAILURE IS NOT THE OPPOSITE OF SUCCESS: IT'S PART OF SUCCESS.

. . . .

CHANGE YOUR THOUGHTS AND YOU CHANGE YOUR WORLD.
#OTB

DESTINY IS NO MATTER OF CHANCE. IT IS A MATTER OF CHOICE. IT IS NOT A THING TO BE WAITED FOR; IT IS A THING TO BE ACHIEVED.

#OTB

FOCUS ON BEING PRODUCTIVE INSTEAD OF BUSY.

. . . .

DON'T LET ANYONE TELL YOU THERE IS SOMETHING YOU CAN'T DO. IF YOU HAVE A DREAM, PROTECT IT. IF YOU WANT SOMETHING, GO GET IT.
#OTB

DEFINITENESS OF PURPOSE IS THE STARTING POINT OF ALL ACHIEVEMENT.

....

DIRECTION IS SO MUCH MORE IMPORTANT THAN SPEED. MANY PEOPLE ARE GOING NOWHERE FAST.
DO IT FIRST OR DO IT DIFFERENTLY.
#OTB

LOVE THE FIRST "NO". LET THAT FIRST "NO" GIVE YOU THE PREMISE FOR ADJUSTING AND CORRECTING TO GET TO THE END GOAL.

. . . .

DIFFICULTIES INCREASE THE NEARER WE APPROACH THE GOAL.
#OTB

FALL SEVEN TIMES AND STAND UP EIGHT.

. . . .

THE ONE WHO FALLS AND GETS UP IS MUCH STRONGER THAN THE ONE WHO NEVER FELL.
#OTB

YOU ONLY LIVE ONCE, BUT IF YOU DO IT RIGHT, ONCE IS ENOUGH.

....

SACRIFICE COMES BEFORE SUCCESS.

#OTB

SHOOT FOR THE MOON. EVEN IF YOU MISS, YOU'LL LAND AMONG THE STARS.

....

SET A GOAL SO BIG THAT YOU CAN'T ACHIEVE IT UNTIL YOU GROW INTO THE PERSON WHO CAN.
#OTB

SOLVE YOUR PROBLEMS
LIKE A CROSSWORD PUZZLE.
ANSWER THE EASIEST FIRST,
THEN YOU WILL
HAVE A CLUE HOW TO SOLVE
THE DIFFICULT ONES.

. . . .

IF YOU'RE ON
TIME, YOU'RE LATE.

#OTB

DON'T PRACTICE UNTIL YOU GET IT RIGHT. PRACTICE UNTIL YOU CAN'T GET IT WRONG.

. . . .

WHEN SOMETHING ISN'T RIGHT IN YOUR LIFE, CHANGE IT. IMMEDIATELY.
#OTB

STAY POSITIVE, WORK HARD, MAKE IT HAPPEN.

....

STOP FOR A SECOND AND THINK ABOUT HOW AMAZING IT IS GOING TO FEEL WHEN YOU ACHIEVE EVERYTHING YOU ARE WORKING HARD FOR RIGHT NOW.
#OTB

OPPORTUNITIES DON'T JUST HAPPEN; YOU CREATE THEM.

. . . .

I FIND THAT THE HARDER I WORK, THE MORE LUCK I SEEM TO HAVE.
#OTB

IF YOU CAN'T STOP THINKING ABOUT IT, DON'T STOP WORKING FOR IT.

. . . .

IF YOU DO WHAT YOU ALWAYS DID, YOU WILL GET WHAT YOU ALWAYS GOT.
#OTB

LET YOUR DREAMS BE BIGGER
THAN YOUR FEARS AND YOUR
ACTIONS BE BIGGER
THAN YOUR WORDS.

. . . .

IF YOU'RE NOT WILLING TO
RISK THE USUAL, YOU'LL
HAVE TO SETTLE FOR
THE ORDINARY.
#OTB

IT IS A MOST MORTIFYING REFLECTION FOR A MAN TO CONSIDER WHAT HE HAS DONE, COMPARED TO WHAT HE MIGHT HAVE DONE.

....

IT'S BETTER TO FAIL IN ORIGINALITY THAN TO SUCCEED IN IMITATION.
#OTB

IT'S NEVER TOO LATE TO BE WHAT YOU MIGHT HAVE BEEN.

....

TAKE TIME FOR YOURSELF AND FIGURE OUT WHAT EXCITES YOU AND MOTIVATES YOU.
#OTB

IN ORDER TO BE SUCCESSFUL, YOUR FOCUS HAS TO BE SO INTENSE PEOPLE THINK YOU'RE CRAZY.

· ·

THE MOST IMPORTANT QUESTION TO ASK IS, WHAT AM I BECOMING?

· ·

TAKE CARE OF YOUR BODY. IT'S THE ONLY PLACE YOU HAVE TO LIVE.

#OTB

**IF YOU CAN IMAGINE IT,
YOU CAN ACHIEVE IT.
IF YOU CAN DREAM IT,
YOU CAN BECOME IT.
MAKE YOUR OWN DESTINY.**

....

**WHAT YOU THINK, YOU BECOME.
WHAT YOU FEEL, YOU ATTRACT.
WHAT YOU IMAGINE, YOU CREATE.**
#OTB

IF YOU CAN SEE IT IN
YOUR MIND, YOU CAN HOLD IT
IN YOUR HANDS.

. . . .

THINK YOURSELF AS A
HUMAN MAGNET —
CONSTANTLY ATTRACTING
WHAT YOU SPEAK,
THINK AND FEEL.
#OTB

DON'T FORGET TO CELEBRATE THE SMALL VICTORIES.

. . . .

SUCCESS HAPPENS AFTER A SERIES OF SMALL WINS.
#OTB

ALWAYS WORK LIKE YOU HAVE SOMETHING TO PROVE.

· ·

MAKE THE REST OF YOUR LIFE THE BEST OF YOUR LIFE.

#OTB

WHAT'S THE POINT OF BEING ALIVE IF YOU DON'T AT LEAST TRY TO DO SOMETHING REMARKABLE?

....

DON'T COUNT THE DAYS; MAKE THE DAYS COUNT.
#OTB

FORGET ALL THE REASONS WHY IT WON'T WORK AND BELIEVE THE ONE REASON WHY IT WILL.

....

WHATEVER YOU CAN DO, OR DREAM YOU CAN, BEGIN IT. BOLDNESS HAS GENIUS, POWER AND MAGIC IN IT.

#OTB

YOU MISS 100% OF THE SHOTS YOU DON'T TAKE.

· ·

IF YOU AIM AT NOTHING, YOU WILL HIT IT EVERY TIME.
#OTB

IF YOU DON'T GO AFTER IT, YOU WILL NEVER HAVE IT.

. . . .

LEARN HOW TO CREATE MULTIPLE STREAMS OF INCOME WHILE LIVING LIFE TO THE MAX.
#OTB

THERE IS NO FORMULA FOR SUCCESS, BUT THERE IS A FORMULA FOR FAILURE, WHICH IS: TRY TO PLEASE EVERYBODY.

THOSE WHO THINK YOU'RE LUCKY HAVEN'T SEEN HOW HARD YOU'VE WORKED.

#OTB

IMAGINE YOUR LIFE IS PERFECT IN EVERY RESPECT; WHAT WOULD IT LOOK LIKE?

· ·

HAPPINESS BEGINS WITH YOU. NOT YOUR RELATIONSHIP, YOUR FRIENDS, OR YOUR JOB — BUT WITH YOU.
#OTB

LIFE IS TOO SHORT TO WORRY ABOUT STUPID THINGS. HAVE FUN. REGRET NOTHING, AND DON'T LET PEOPLE BRING YOU DOWN.

....

HAPPINESS IS A JOURNEY, NOT A DESTINATION.
#OTB

TAKE A REST. A FIELD THAT HAS RESTED YIELDS A BEAUTIFUL CROP.

. . . .

YOU'VE GOT TO GET UP EVERY MORNING WITH DETERMINATION IF YOU'RE GOING TO GO TO BED WITH SATISFACTION.
#OTB

NO ONE WILL EVER GIVE YOU PERMISSION TO LIVE YOUR DREAMS.

. . . .

THE QUESTION ISN'T WHO IS GOING TO LET ME; IT'S WHO IS GOING TO STOP ME.

#OTB

HAVE THE COURAGE TO FOLLOW YOUR HEART AND INTUITION. THEY ALREADY KNOW WHAT YOU TRULY WANT TO BECOME.

....

IF YOU FAIL TO PREPARE, PREPARE TO FAIL.
#OTB

STRIVE FOR PROGRESS, NOT PERFECTION.

·························

YOU DON'T HAVE TO BE GREAT TO START, BUT YOU HAVE TO START TO BE GREAT.
#OTB

THERE IS NO PASSION TO BE FOUND PLAYING SMALL.
#OTB

THIS IS YOUR LIFE. DO WHAT YOU LOVE, AND DO IT OFTEN. IF YOU DON'T LIKE SOMETHING, CHANGE IT.

LET WHAT YOU LOVE BE WHAT YOU DO.

NEVER LET ORDINARY PEOPLE TELL YOU THAT YOU CAN'T LIVE AN EXTRAORDINARY LIFE.
#OTB

LIFE IS SHORT. LIVE YOUR DREAM AND SHARE YOUR PASSION.

· ·

LOVE IT WHEN PEOPLE DOUBT YOU. USE IT TO MAKE YOURSELF WORK HARDER TO PROVE THEM WRONG.
#OTB

THERE WILL BE HATERS, THERE WILL BE DOUBTERS, THERE WILL BE NON-BELIEVERS, AND THEN THERE WILL BE YOU PROVING THEM ALL WRONG.
#OTB

A TIGER DOESN'T LOSE SLEEP OVER THE OPINION OF A SHEEP.

. . . .

DON'T LET THE FEAR OF LOSING BE GREATER THAN THE EXCITEMENT OF WINNING.
#OTB

IF YOU LOOK AT WHAT YOU HAVE IN LIFE, YOU'LL ALWAYS HAVE MORE. IF YOU LOOK AT WHAT YOU DON'T HAVE IN LIFE, YOU'LL NEVER HAVE ENOUGH.

· ·

IF YOU DON'T HAVE WHAT YOU WANT, GO GET IT.
#OTB

NEVER LOSE. EITHER WIN OR LEARN.

IF IT DOESN'T CHALLENGE YOU, IT WON'T CHANGE YOU.

DREAM BIG. WAKE UP. HUSTLE. REPEAT.
#OTB

IF THE PLAN DOESN'T WORK, CHANGE THE PLAN BUT NEVER THE GOAL.

. . . .

DON'T RUN FROM PRESSURE, EMBRACE IT, WELCOME IT. PRESSURE IS A PRIVILEGE THAT ALLOWS YOU TO DO SOMETHING EXTRAORDINARY.
#OTB

PEOPLE WILL FORGET WHAT YOU
SAID, PEOPLE WILL FORGET WHAT
YOU DID, BUT PEOPLE WILL
NEVER FORGET HOW YOU
MADE THEM FEEL.

A GOOD LIFE IS WHEN YOU SMILE
OFTEN, DREAM BIG, LAUGH
A LOT AND REALISE HOW
BLESSED YOU ARE FOR
WHAT YOU HAVE.
#OTB

A MAN WHO DARES TO WASTE ONE HOUR OF LIFE HAS NOT DISCOVERED THE VALUE OF LIFE.

. . . .

THE TIME YOU ENJOY WASTING IS NOT WASTED TIME.
#OTB

YOUR TIME IS LIMITED, SO DON'T WASTE IT LIVING SOMEONE ELSE'S LIFE.

. . . .

YOU LIVE LONGER ONCE YOU REALISE THAT TIME SPENT BEING UNHAPPY IS WASTED.
#OTB

BE MINDFUL OF HOW YOU APPROACH TIME. WATCHING THE CLOCK IS NOT THE SAME AS WATCHING THE SUN RISE.

. . . .

BE THE CHANGE THAT YOU WISH TO SEE IN THE WORLD.
#OTB

A WISE PERSON DOES AT ONCE,
WHAT A FOOL DOES AT LAST.
BOTH DO THE SAME THING; ONLY
AT DIFFERENT TIMES.

. . . .

BE THE EXAMPLE YOUR KIDS
NEED TO SUCCEED.
#OTB

A TRULY RICH MAN IS ONE WHOSE
CHILDREN RUN INTO HIS ARMS
WHEN HIS HANDS ARE EMPTY.

. . . .

LIFE IS ABOUT MAKING AN
IMPACT, NOT MAKING AN
INCOME.
#OTB

TRY NOT TO BECOME A PERSON OF SUCCESS, BUT RATHER TRY TO BECOME A PERSON OF VALUE.

THE TWO MOST IMPORTANT FORMS OF CURRENCY IN LIFE ARE KNOWLEDGE AND RESPECT.
#OTB

ALWAYS FIGHT THE GOOD FIGHT.

· ·

IT'S BETTER TO STARVE THAN EAT JUST WHATEVER; AND BETTER TO BE ALONE THAN JUST WITH WHOMEVER.
#OTB

LIFE IS 10% WHAT HAPPENS TO YOU AND 90% OF HOW YOU REACT TO IT.

....

CERTAIN THINGS CATCH YOUR EYE, BUT PURSUE ONLY THOSE THAT CAPTURE THE HEART.

#OTB

LOOK TO THE FUTURE, BECAUSE THAT IS WHERE YOU'LL SPEND THE REST OF YOUR LIFE.

. . . .

EVERYTHING WILL BE GOOD IN THE END. IF IT'S NOT GOOD, IT IS NOT THE END.
#OTB

DECIDE. COMMIT. ACT. SUCCEED. REPEAT.

BE RELENTLESS. PERSEVERE. NEVER GIVE UP.

IT'S UP TO YOU.
#OTB

A MAN CAN BE AS GREAT AS HE
WANTS TO BE.
IF YOU BELIEVE IN YOURSELF AND
HAVE THE COURAGE,
THE DETERMINATION, THE
DEDICATION, THE COMPETITIVE
DRIVE AND IF YOU ARE
WILLING TO SACRIFICE
THE LITTLE THINGS IN LIFE
AND PAY THE PRICE FOR THE
THINGS THAT ARE WORTHWHILE,
IT CAN BE DONE.
#OTB

WHEN YOU'RE THROWN TO THE WOLVES, COME BACK LEADING THE PACK.

....

WORK HARD. PLAY HARD. LIVE HARDER.

....

MAKE THE REST OF YOUR LIFE THE BEST OF YOUR LIFE.
#OTB

MAP OUT YOUR FUTURE, BUT DO IT IN PENCIL.

....

THIS YEAR SOMEONE WILL MAKE THEIR DREAM COME TRUE.
MAKE SURE IT'S YOU.
#OTB

KNOW YOUR LIMITS, BUT NEVER STOP TRYING TO EXCEED THEM.

....

ONCE YOU BECOME FEARLESS, LIFE BECOMES LIMITLESS.

....

FINO ALLA FINE.
#OTB

DEAR HATERS, THERE'S SO MUCH MORE FOR YOU TO BE MAD AT — JUST BE PATIENT.

#OTB

Acknowledgements

I'd like to extend my appreciation to a great group of friends who contributed some of the sayings and quotes in this book: Zach, Mark, Mahdi, Nayef, Jules, Farhad, Cesare, Tal, Tommy, Joe, Aaron, Lisa, Nate, Rita, Johnatan, Janette, Jaak, Michael, Momo, and others.

My special appreciation goes out to Matteo, a dear friend and hard worker. It was he who motivated me to discover and learn what #OTB truly means, and embrace it in my own life.

www.ingramcontent.com/pod-product-compliance
Lightning Source LLC
LaVergne TN
LVHW051413080426
835508LV00022B/3057